First edition for the United States
and Canada published in 2014
by Barron's Educational Series, Inc.

First published in 2014- by Wayland
Text copyright © Pat Thomas 2014
Illustrations copyright © Wayland 2014

Wayland is a division of Hachette Children's Books,
a Hachette UK company.
www.hachette.co.uk

Concept design: Kate Buxton
Series design: Paul Cherrill for Basement68
Editor: Victoria Brooker

All inquiries should be addressed to:
Barron's Educational Series, Inc.
250 Wireless Boulevard
Hauppauge, New York 11788
www.barronseduc.com

ISBN: 978-1-4380-0471-6

Library of Congress Control Number: 2013957084

Date of manufacture: May 2014
Manufactured by: WKT Co. Ltd., Guangdang, China

Printed in China

9 8 7 6 5 4 3 2 1

Don't Call Me Fat!

A FIRST LOOK AT BEING OVERWEIGHT

PAT THOMAS
ILLUSTRATED BY CLAIRE KEAY

There are lots of things we all do
every day to stay healthy.

We take baths, brush our teeth,
run around and play, and get
plenty of sleep. We also
try to eat well.

Good food helps us grow and gives
us energy. It can make us stronger
and smarter and healthier.

But it's important to eat just the right amount.

If we eat too little we can be too thin and feel hungry and weak. But if we eat too much, we can feel heavy and tired.

What about you?

What kinds of foods do you like to eat? Can you name some foods that are good for you and some foods that are not so good for you?

Eating too much is like putting too much air in a tire – or too many clothes in your suitcase.

It can slow you down
and stop your body from
working the way it should.

People eat too much for lots of reasons
- and not just because they are hungry.

They eat because they are bored, or sad, or because their
family or friends are eating and they want to join in.

Trying to eat less can be hard when there are so many ads and commercials everywhere showing us different foods and telling us to eat more!

What about you?

Do you know some people who eat too much? When you see ads for food, do they make you feel hungry?

It doesn't matter whether you are a child or an adult, weighing more than is healthy can stop you from doing fun things like running, jumping, swimming, and climbing as far and as fast as others.

It can make it hard to find clothes that feel comfortable. And it can make you feel as if you are very different from others and that you don't fit in.

None of these things are true.
No one can tell what a person is like
just by what size they are.

Whatever size we are, we all have special talents and skills – being overweight doesn't change that.

What about you?

What sorts of things are you good at? What do you enjoy doing? Are there any new things you'd like to try?

Sometimes when you are overweight, people will try to make you feel bad about it.

They may try to stop you from sitting next to them or playing games with them...

...or tease or bully you because you are not the same as them. Teasing or bullying people for how they look is mean and is never the right thing to do.

People who are overweight
are not greedy or lazy.

Often they just need someone like their
friends or family or teachers to help them learn
how to take care of themselves by eating
less and exercising more.

Learning to eat the right foods, to stop eating when you are full, and to exercise more is like learning to do anything else.

It takes practice and patience, and you need lots of people around you who can help you to get better at it.

If you have friends or other members
of your family who are overweight,
you can all practice together...

...and help
each other to
say "no thank
you" to foods
that look nice but aren't
very good for you.

It's much easier to stay healthy when we all help and support one another.

Your body can do amazing
things and take you to amazing places
if you take care of it.

Eating just the right amount
of healthy food is a good way to
make sure you enjoy yourself
along the way.

HOW TO USE THIS BOOK

The purpose of this book is to help parents and young children have their first discussions about food and health. Children have to learn about healthy eating the same way they have to learn about other things—through repetition and positive reinforcement. The questions in the "What about you?" sections can be useful prompts for understanding things from your child's point of view.

Parents are in charge. Young children do not make independent decisions about what to eat, or how much to eat, or when to eat. Nor are they in charge of their own social and exercise schedules. Very few children can lose weight without parental support, so do what you can to help set in stone healthy habits that will last a lifetime.

Choose your words carefully. Emotionally charged discussions about weight aren't appropriate at any time, but in young children they risk making them far too self-conscious. Very young children are generally not too concerned with what they look like until someone tells them otherwise. Focus on positives, for instance on the ways that healthy food makes you feel stronger and makes your brain smarter.

Put it in context. Instead of big overwhelming conversations, use time together—for instance, when food shopping, casually discuss why you are choosing one food over another or the health benefits of certain foods.

Sensible portions. For very young children, sensible portions of healthy foods is the best way to begin to manage weight problems. Use this book to help them understand the concept of "enough" and how it can help them feel better and have more energy.

It's a family affair. Children imitate their parents' eating and exercise habits, and being overweight does tend to run in families.

To encourage your child to get up and move, make getting healthy a family project where everyone can join in. Special activities just for kids, such as the Saturday gym or swimming, are great. But regular activities that the whole family can enjoy are also a good way of encouraging your child to value being active.

Cut TV time. Reducing the amount of time your child spends watching TV has two big benefits. It helps direct them into more active pastimes, and it also reduces their exposure to TV commercials for unhealthy foods. Studies show that commercials have a big influence on children's eating habits. When watching TV, you can help by discussing why certain foods are not healthy and why you don't buy them for your family.

Healthy snacks. Children need to eat. Unless advised by a medical professional for a pressing health reason, young children should not diet and snacks should not be denied them if they are genuinely hungry. Make sure you have healthy snacks like fruit or vegetables on hand at home. Likewise, some schools have found that introducing a "fruit time" in the afternoon is a great time to talk about healthy foods and their effects on the body, such as how fruit or vegetables can improve energy levels and help to reinforce good eating habits.

Schools projects. Schools are well placed to teach about diet and fitness from many different angles—and to enforce a zero tolerance policy on bullying and teasing. Exploring the foods people from other cultures consider healthy can broaden children's horizons considerably. Class projects on food and portion sizes are also important. Similarly, introducing a wide range of PE or playground activities can aid children in finding a sport which suits them.

BOOKS TO READ

For children

Hamster Camp: How Harry Got Fit
Teresa Bateman
(Albert Whitman & Company, 2005)

Healthy and Happy: Eating Well
Robyn Hardyman
(Wayland, 2011)

Looking After Me: Eating Well
Liz Gogerly and Mike Gordon
(Wayland, 2013)

Mini and Me: Learning Healthy Habits
Shelly Stockum, Sandi Stewart, Greg Stockum
(Jabberwocky Books, 2009)

For parents

Your Child's Weight: Helping Without Harming
Ellyn Satter
(Kelcy Press, 2005)

Red Light, Green Light, Eat Right: The Food Solution That Lets Kids Be Kids
Joanna Dolgoff
(Rodale Books, 2009)

How to Raise a Healthy Child in Spite of Your Doctor
Robert Mendelsohn
(Ballantine Books, Inc. 1987)

RESOURCES FOR ADULTS

www.cdc.gov/healthyweight/children/

Advice for parents on how to help overweight children.

www.nhs.uk/change4life/Pages/change-for-life.aspx

A website giving advice on how to start eating healthily and getting more exercise for families.

www.webmd.com/parenting/raising-fit-kids/weight/safe-weight-loss

A WebMD resource to help families make sensible changes that benefit overweight children.